Ireland's Beautiful Places

With Traditional Sayings

MICHAEL SHAW

Fresh Squeezed Publishing

RICHMOND, VIRGINIA

Copyright © 2015, 2019 by Michael Shaw

All rights reserved. No part of this publication may be reproduced, distributed or transmitted in any form or by any means, without prior written permission.

Michael Shaw /Fresh Squeezed Publishing
www.mikeshawtoday.com

Publisher's Note: To obtain the free full color version of this book in the e-format you desire, check the instructions in the back of this book.

This is a work of fiction. Names, characters, places, and incidents are a product of the author's imagination. Locales and public names are sometimes used for atmospheric purposes. Photos have been altered so that any resemblance to actual people, living or dead, or to businesses, companies, events, institutions, or locales is completely coincidental.

Cover photo: Boat at Ring of Kerry

Ireland's Beautiful Places/ Michael Shaw -- 2nd ed.
ISBN 978-1522901174

To those who are,
and all who want to be...
Irish!

Contents

Preface 7

Gratitude 9

Character 15

Friendship 25

Knowledge 31

Thrift 39

Wisdom 47

Travelogue 59

Screenplay Synopsis 69

Preface

WHEN YOU VISIT IRELAND, you'll discover not only many things about the place and its people, but you will feel transported to a different state of being. There is some magic in a visit to Ireland, and at times you even lose a sense of what century you are in.

We found the people of Ireland to be generous and welcoming, and we especially enjoyed their humor. We observed universal respect for thrift and prudence balanced by the offer of hospitality and friendship. The young people thirst for knowledge while elders have a reverence for wisdom and, above all, character. We've touched on these themes in this book by using separate chapters.

The format of this book a mix of travel photography coupled with traditional Irish sayings. It's our way to give you a feeling for the beauty of the country and its landmarks, as well as a way to allow the Irish people to speak for themselves.

We hope this book gets you started making your travel plans, and we're sure you will enjoy a visit to Ireland as much as we did!

—Mike & Donna

1

Gratitude

DONNA WAS THRILLED to have an opportunity to go to Ireland, the homeland of her ancestors. Before our trip, she spent many weeks tracing her genealogy on her grandmother's side.

Prior to this adventure, Donna barely knew her lineage, and she was certainly unable to fathom what life must have been like for her ancestors. Only while exploring their lands, their burial places, and what remained of their homes and castles, she began to understand what they and all the Irish went through while trying to survive daily life amidst political turmoil.

As we drove around Ireland we both felt as if we were home. While this vacation may have brought us back to a much simpler time, reducing stress from our daily lives, we also realized how blessed we are in this present era.

This chapter is about gratitude. We are grateful for the political freedom, the spiritual and social diversity, and the economic abundance we enjoy today.

He who has water and peat on his own farm has the world his own way.

There are finer fish in the sea than have ever been caught.

Never dread the winter till the snow is on the blanket.

A heavy purse makes a light heart.

The older the fiddle the sweeter the tune.

Irelands Beautiful Places

Many a day shall we rest in the clay.

The man with a cow doesn't need a scythe.

However long the day, night must fall.

2

Character

SOMEONE ONCE TOLD me, "There are two kinds of people: those who are Irish, and those who want to be Irish." That day, I had to face up to it, I am the latter. So I made it my task to find out what it is to be Irish. After doing some research on my own, it was pretty easy to convince Donna to go on a vacation to Ireland to achieve my goal.

Before the trip, we listened to Irish songs. Music is one good way to know the character of a people. Anyone who has ever listened to *Danny Boy* or *Finnegan's Wake* will begin to sense the complexity of what it is to be Irish. One song is an emotionally stirring account of a son's last visit to his father, the other a hilarious tale of a raucous fight over a corpse at a funeral. Both reveal a great deal about the character of the Irish. We get the sense that for the Irish, life and death are similar in some mysterious way, to be celebrated equally.

Irish films also help describe the character of the people. Donna and I watched all the movies we could find, one about a greyhound dog, another a leap year love story, we watched movies about Irish Cieli bands, and those about weddings, wakes and funerals. We took great pleasure in all the drama, humor, and romantic comedy. We learned also of legends and superstitions. Not all Irish people believe leprechauns, four leaf clovers, and pots of gold at the end of the rainbow.

To truly know the character of the people, however, one must visit the country itself, see its landmarks, castles, and vistas. Even more importantly, one must see the homes of ordinary people with their universally well-kept gardens and stone work. One must indulge too in Irish food and drink in order to taste the Irish temperament. There is good why reason people consider a visit to Bushmills distillery and the Guinness brewery as essential stops in their tours.

Finally, in our travels, our biggest surprise was the consistently high level of culinary art—in even the simplest meals. Whether at a restaurant or roadside café, even at a petrol station convenience store—meals, soups, salads, snacks, pastries and muffins alike, everything is prepared and served with much care. The food is always fresh because it is locally sourced. The country is small geographically and we imagine there must be a sense of community among cooks and chefs, each striving to be the best. That's how it seems to us.

Did I find out what it is to be Irish, without actually being Irish? I think I came pretty close, and I know I had a blast trying to figure it all out.

Irelands Beautiful Places 17

Better good manners than good looks.

Who keeps his tongue keeps his friends.

A combed head sells the feet.

Irelands Beautiful Places 19

Better the trouble that follows death than the trouble that follows shame.

Better to be a man of character than a man of means.

Even a tin knocker will shine on a dirty door.

Every branch blossoms according to the root from which it sprung.

It's a dirty bird that won't keep its own nest clean.

The work praises the man.

Irelands Beautiful Places 23

They are scarce of news that speak ill of their mother.

Unwillingness easily finds an excuse.

It is more difficult to maintain honour than to become prosperous.

If you want praise, die. If you want blame, marry.

3

Friendship

A MAJOR DISCOVERY we made in Ireland was how well Mike and I travel together. With all the planning involved, at first Mike didn't act very excited about the trip. It was like I was his travel agent, and he was going on a business trip. Yet by the end of our vacation, we had established a wonderful friendship which became deeper because of the journey.

They say that the best way to test a relationship is to take a road trip together. Mike kept driving on the right side of the road which, in Ireland, is the wrong side of the road. He nearly killed us a dozen times over. He would often drive quickly into one-way exits and he would ignore construction signs which neither of us understood. And the roads are so narrow, we had many near head-on collisions. I did a lot of screaming. In a good way.

Despite the harrowing travel throughout our trip, the high level of stress experienced by Mike while driving, and the adrenaline induced nightmares I experienced, we grew closer in our relationship. We discovered even more intensely all the little things that make a vacation enjoyable such as a moonlit bay at a spa resort, storm clouds over a windmill on the coast, and walking Dublin's city streets at night. We went to Ireland with a mindset of travel companions, and came home as best friends.

Better fifty enemies outside the house than one within.

The person bringing good news knocks boldly on the door.

Ireland's Beautiful Places

No two people ever lit a fire without disagreeing.

A cat can look at a king.

An oak is often split by a wedge from its own branch.

Ireland's Beautiful Places 29

It is not the same to go to the king's house as to come from it.

It's for her own good that the cat purrs.

The old dog for the hard road and leave the pup on the path.

4

Knowledge

BEFORE OUR TRIP, Donna did historical research and read books about her Irish ancestry. She created genealogical charts and family trees. By researching the places of her great-great grandparents, she was able to set up a meaningful travel route for us because she had gained a better understanding of the places we'd visit.

I did political research and wrote an original screenplay about the violence in Ireland between the IRA and the Nationalists. Before going there, writing a film script actually helped me understand the religious and political divisions in Ireland. (A synopsis of this screen drama—with an underlying romance—is in the back of this book as its own chapter.)

While Donna was to visit every place of her ancestors, I insisted we go to all the towns mentioned in the Irish pub songs which I had been singing to in my car. She dutifully planned every detail, booked the flights and hotels, and mapped a route assured to accommodate us both. Our visit to The Emerald Isle would include town and country, churches and pubs, farms and museums, stone castles and coastal cliffs.

We would rent a car, and all I had to do was drive.

Questioning is the door of knowledge.

You won't learn to swim on the kitchen floor.

*If it's drowning you're after,
don't torment yourself with shallow water.*

If you don't want flour on your clothes, stay out of the mill.

Every man's mind is his kingdom.

As the old cock crows, the young cock learns.

Ireland's Beautiful Places 37

If your messenger is slow, go to meet him.

The schoolhouse bell sounds bitter in youth and sweet in old age.

5

Thrift

WHEN WE ARRIVED, the first thing I did was destroy our rental car. First, I couldn't figure out how to put it in reverse. No, I didn't ram it into the pole. I adjusted the gear shift lever to the *R* for reverse, looked behind me to back up, pressed the accelerator gently and I slowly, methodically, drove it inch-by-inch into a concrete pole.

Once on the road, the vehicle still quite operable, I then burnt out the clutch. This, all somewhere in Dublin between the airport and our hotel. In life we all experience a few unforgettable smells. Fresh baked bread, baby powder, and for me, high on the list now, is the smell of a burnt out clutch.

I forgot to mention the hand brake had been on the entire time, so that was burnt out too. Apparently, the cars there have a button not a lever for the handbrake, and that's what the red light must've been indicating.

To the rental car people, again, I'm truly sorry. I am wiser now. Please forgive me.

My advice for Americans: Spend the extra money and rent an automatic transmission vehicle to start with. It is more expensive to get a replacement after you burn out the clutch on your first rental. Thrift is what this chapter is about.

Many a sudden change takes place on an unlikely day.

You never miss the water till the well runs dry.

Ireland's Beautiful Places 41

Better be sparing at first than at last.

If you buy what you don't need you might have to sell what you do.

If you move old furniture it may fall to bits.

There is no luck except where there is discipline.

Keep your shop and your shop will keep you.

Ireland's Beautiful Places

Only a fool burns his coal without warming himself.

6

Wisdom

WISDOM, UNLIKE KNOWLEDGE, isn't acquired instantly. Wisdom comes with time, and usually a good amount of suffering. For an individual it takes many years, for a country it may require many centuries to mature and become wise.

We know that in ancient times, local clans in Ireland fought nomads and invaders bitterly for territory and survival. Since the 1500's, people of Ireland had a love-hate relationship with the English, divided along political and religious lines.

Thankfully, The Republic of Ireland and Northern Ireland have come to terms, and Ireland, that incredibly beautiful island in the North Atlantic, is populated by an Irish people. Clearly they have taken to heart the wisdom found in their own sayings.

This wisdom has always existed in Gaelic culture, and abounds in Irish music and literature. It is also a wisdom shared culturally with Great Britain. The imagined differences become less important by the day as forgiveness grows in everyone's hearts. Such is wisdom.

Melodious is the closed mouth.

Do not resent growing old. Many are denied the privilege.

Ireland's Beautiful Places 49

Blow not on dead embers.

Life is a strange lad.

Continual cheerfulness is a sign of wisdom.

No time for health today, no health for your time tomorrow.

*Young people don't know what old age is,
and old people forget what youth was.*

Earth has no sorrows that heaven cannot heal.

A good retreat is better than a bad stand.

A questioning man is halfway to being wise.

Ireland's Beautiful Places 55

Lose an hour in the morning and you'll be looking for it all day.

Silence is the fence around the haggard where wisdom is stacked.

Ireland's Beautiful Places 57

What I am afraid to hear I'd better say first myself.

7

Travelogue

BELOW IS A LIST of the photos in order of appearance throughout the book. The format is chapter heading, photo title, place, and description of the location. All photos taken August and September 2014 by Michael and Donna Shaw.

GRATITUDE

Sheep on a Small Farm – Enniskillen, County Fermanagh – We stayed at Corrigans Shore House, a bed and breakfast farm on the Lough Erne River. Great place to stay. Excellent early morning photography. Eniskillen Castle in town is nice place to have an evening stroll at sunset along Lough Erne. The Clancy Brothers, The Chieftains, and The Dubliners have songs mentioning the town.

Sunset on Lough Foyle - Redcastle, County Donegal – Photo taken at the Redcastle Oceanfront Spa Hotel and Resort on this peninsula on the Irish Sea. We had a wonderful corner room with a view from two sides.

Chimneys in Balbriggan - Balbriggan, County Dublin – A telephoto lens compresses the chimneys for a dramatic effect. Morning fog adds to the Old World feeling. We stayed at the Brackencourt Hotel. The breakfast buffet was extraordinary, reasonably priced when added to the room, and the gingerbread cookies were to die for—homemade from scratch, of course.

Wrought Iron and Gold Gate - Powerscourt Gardens, County Wicklow - Donna's ancestral home in the early 1600's, the family O'Toole. Her family was forced out and the home was turned over to the Wingfields who were well connected to the English government. One of the top gardens in Ireland, voted by National Geographic as the No. 3 garden in the world.

Dublin Door in Yellow– Dublin City- near St. Stephen's Green. Take the bus to this wonderful park and you'll see lots of these brightly colored doors in the Grafton Street area. We got the daily hop-on-hop-off bus pass which allows you to take unlimited tour-buses around the city all day. You get on and off at whichever part of the city you like.

Marble Hall - Powerscourt Estate, County Wicklow - Voted one of the top ten houses and mansions in the world by *Lonely Planet Guide*. Built in the 1700's the house was originally a 13th century castle. This was Donna's ancestors' home in the early 1600s. See above note in Powerscourt Gardens. We enjoyed walking through the gigantic marble hall. A number of motion pictures were filmed here.

White Cow and Calf - Cahir, County Tipperary – Cahir Castle. This is one of Ireland's largest and best preserved castles (built 1142). It is situated on the River Suir, and they have excellent tours. Behind the castle is a farm where I took this photo of a cow and its calf.

Full Moon Rising – Belfast, Northern Ireland – Moonrise over the River Lagan in downtown Belfast. We stayed at the Hilton, and this photo was taken from our hotel-room window. We walked to the Titanic Museum along the scenic river.

CHARACTER

Boat in Dry-dock – Belfast, Northern Ireland – At a local shipyard near the Titanic museum.

Windmill in a Storm – Blennerville, Co. Kerry – This five-storey windmill is the only commercially operating windmill in Ireland and the tallest in Europe of this type. It is located in the Tralee Ship Canal.

Barbershop in Balbriggan - Balbriggan, County Dublin - Like many of our people pictures, this was taken from our very high hotel room window at the Brackencourt Hotel. The hotel is situated on an angle at a busy corner. When photographing people from above, their faces are often obscured, protecting their identity.

Ancient Burial Mound – Knowth, County Meath – The complex of prehistoric stones and burial mounds is the world's oldest astronomical observatory (about 5,000 years old). This photo is of one of the smaller mounds. The Great Mound has two passages east and west which align perfectly with the equinoxes as well as with lunar alignments. The surrounding Neolithic stones contain astronomical drawings too.

Man atop Basalt Columns - Giant's Causeway, County Antrim – This is one of the world's most unique natural wonders. About 40,000 interlocking basalt columns, hexagonal in shape, were formed volcanically about 60 million years ago. Since the columns seem to form steps as they ascend from the sea, the name Giant's Causeway is appropriate and legend tells that the giant's name was Finn MacCool.

Moon over Lough Foyle - Inishowen, County Donegal – Our hotel had a fabulous view of the lake and coastline. We highly recommend the Redcastle Hotel and Spa. They have the most relaxing spa-type pool with built in water jets in different configurations all around the sides of the pool.

Flowers at St. Stephen's Green – Dublin City – This is a city park in the center of town, surrounded by major traffic arteries. Outside the park, artists and photographers display their work. Inside, are statues, Georgian garden squares, a gazebo and bandstand, a fountain and lakes.

Crow at Powerscourt Gardens - Powerscourt Estate, County Wicklow – The crows in Ireland seemed quite unafraid and were huge. Allow at least two hours for walking around the gardens.

Tower at Monasterboice – Monasterboice Cemetery, County Louth - This Irish and Celtic cemetery of ruins from 521 AD is known for its tall round tower and tall crosses. The "Tall Cross" is the tallest in existence, 21 feet tall. The 18 foot cross is described below.

Newspaper Salesman - Dublin Airport, Dublin - We stayed at the Hilton and had a bird's eye view of the car and pedestrian traffic below. We captured some unique people photos. This one, of a newspaper salesman, depicts a moment in time you might see in any busy city in the world.

Ram on a Hill - Causeway Coastal Route Ireland – The coastal route runs between Derry and Belfast. Along this route we found many scenic stops, and although the roads are narrow, it is possible to pull off to snap a quick photo.

City Hall – Dublin City – Walking around the city at night is a must-do. The party is happening in Temple Bar area, and there are different pubs to sample. If you like night photography, there are many places to set up your tripod and wait for the traffic to expose your picture.

Trim Castle - Trim, County Meath – This is Braveheart's Castle from the movie. The wedding photographer was not too happy about my taking pictures right next to her, however it was too hard to pass up the opportunity to capture the beautiful colors and smiling faces. We wish the bride and groom all happiness and blessings.

FRIENDSHIP

Old Mellifont Abbey – Collon, County Louth – Mellifont Abbey is the home of an active community of monks, founded in 1142 by Saint Malachy. It is Ireland's first Cistercian monastery. This photo is of the nearby ruins of the old abbey.

Dublin Doors – Dublin City – Photo taken near Trinity College. Just take the hop-on-hop-off bus and you'll see lots of these colorful portals.

Arches at Glendalough – Glendalough, County Wicklow - Donna's ancestors' burial grounds. At the monastic site are the ruins of a 12th century cathedral. Within, we found grave markers of Donna's family names. Outside, there were these beautiful arches.

Cat Topiary – Belfast, Northern Ireland - The castle is just near Cave Hill, which is one of the highest places in Belfast, so you can have great views of the city and the lake. At Belfast Castle we discovered a recurring cat theme both in the topiary and in the inlaid tilings.

Tree near Waterford Castle - Waterford, County Cork – The grounds surrounding the castle are extensive. There are walking and nature trails with lots of wildlife. An early morning walk gave us this forest picture.

Waterford Castle - Waterford, County Cork – The castle is actually located on an island to which you must ferry your car in order to visit. We stayed there overnight.

Cat Mosaic - Belfast, Northern Ireland - At Belfast Castle. See above.

Harpist at the Cliffs of Moher – Cliffs of Moher, County Clare – The cliffs run for five miles along the coast with breathtaking views. Walking the steps up to O'Brien's Tower, we met harpist Tina Mulrooney and her little dog. Her music is beautiful and we bought one of her CD's. It was a Mr. Bojangles moment.

KNOWLEDGE

Ruins at Mellifont Abbey – See above

Library at Trinity College – Dublin – Here in the long room, fantastic lighting and views overwhelmed us with opportunities for taking pictures. The 200,000 book library is well known for housing The Book of Kells, which is the 9th century manuscript of the gospels.

River Liffey – Dublin City – The Liffey divides Dublin's north and south sides. The river flows from the Wicklow Mountains, through Dublin downtown, and out to the Irish Sea. This photo taken at night from the bridge at lower O' Connell Street. Ha'Penny Bridge is in the center of the photo.

Windmill at Ballycopeland – Ballycopeland, County Down - We looked all over Ireland and only could find two windmills. This windmill has been restored to full working order. It was built sometime in the 18th or 19th century. The only way to see it is if the people in the Miller's house will allow you. If you drive around the back on Moss Road, there is an asphalt pad on which you can park, and then you can walk across a field, strewn with cow pies, you can get a good view of the windmill.

Magenta Door – Liscannor, County Clare - We stayed at the Logues Liscannor Hotel near the Cliffs of Moher. We sighted this beautiful doorway on our walk to dinner. We had dinner at Vaughan's Anchor Inn, and it was superb. The chef gave us a sample of his butternut squash soup with sage and orange. Fabulous!

Statue and Bell Tower – Dublin –Trinity College is Ireland's oldest university, founded in 1592. Its library holds every book printed in the UK and in Ireland. The famous 100 foot tall, granite Campanile Bell Tower was built in 1853 and donated by the Archbishop of Armagh. The statue depicts Irish writer, historian and political theorist William Edward Hartpole Lecky, M.P. It's a bronze statue unveiled in 1906.

Nighttime Street in Balbriggan - Balbriggan, County Dublin – Photo taken from our hotel window. A simple time-exposure capturing the traffic below. See above references.

Bell Tower – Dublin – The granite Campanile Bell Tower (see above) was built in 1853 and is a wonderful photography subject because there are many interesting views—from the sides, and from underneath it. Students be warned: According to legend, any student who passes underneath the tower when the bells toll shall fail his exams. Some students never walk beneath the tower until they graduate. Little known fact: It is illegal for a student to walk through Trinity College without a sword.

****

THRIFT

Ferry Crossing - Strangford Lough, County Down – There is a ferry which runs between Strangford and Portaferry. We took this ferry to save time as opposed to driving the long coastal route of about 75 kilometers (an hour and a half by car). The ferry takes 8 minutes. Ferry crossings are reasonable in price and have good photo opportunities before, during, and after the ride.

Hexagonal Stones and Tidal Pool - Giant's Causeway, County Antrim – See above entry.

The Spire - Dublin City, Dublin – This sculpture was commissioned as part of a city renewal program, and represents merging of technology and art. It is constructed of stainless steel and was assembled from eight hollow tubes of decreasing diameter. At the base, the spire is about ten feet in diameter, and at the top about six inches. At dark, it seems to merge into the sky. During the day, because of shot peening to the surface, it reflects light.

Vase in Powerscourt Hall - Powerscourt Estate, County Wicklow – In the marble halls are statues and large vases. (See above.)

Christ Church Cathedral - Dublin City, Dublin – This medieval church was founded around 1028 after the Hiberno-Norse king of Dublin made his pilgrimage to Rome. The cathedral was renovated and rebuilt in the late 1870's. The church has 19 bells. This photo is from the top deck of our hop-on-hop-off tour bus.

Seagull - Liscannor, County Clare - Our hotel, Logues Liscannor Hotel was situated in the middle of a little fishing village. It was a perfect place to walk around in the evening and get pictures of seagulls.

Ship's Chandlers – Waterford, County Cork – After our stay at the Waterford Castle Hotel, we went exploring in this island town. On a side street is the famous Waterford Crystal factory, showroom, and store. The streets along the waterfront are picturesque. This photo is one of many shops we photographed.

Irish Writer - Balbriggan, County Dublin - We don't know if this is a real Irish writer, but we'd like to believe it so. The view from our hotel room led us to fascinating stories we made up about all the people passing below. This striding woman with a cigarette and a paperback in her hand made a good visual subject. See above references to our hotel and its view.

****

WISDOM

Kerbstone at Knowth - Knowth, County Meath - Stone with prehistoric carving at the base of the main burial mound in Knowth. See above references to Knowth.

Bathroom Sink - Waterford, County Cork – It's the sink in our hotel room at Waterford Castle Hotel. See above references.

Burial Mound - Newgrange, County Meath - Main burial mound at Newgrange. Quartz façade is a reconstruction by archeologist based upon the placement of what was believed to be the fallen stones. The pattern on the ground seemed to have been made when the stones fell off the dirt wall of the burial mound.

Boy Running - St. Stephen's Green, Dublin – As described earlier, this is a nice park to enjoy for part of the day. Besides the flowers and man-made lakes, there are sculptures to honor of famous personages of Ireland including James Joyce and William Butler Yeats, a fountain representing The Three Fates, and a WW II memorial to *Operation Shamrock* from the German people, thanking Ireland for taking in their children as refugees during the war.

Harpist and Dog - Cliffs of Moher, County Clare – The Cliffs of Moher were formed more than 300 million years ago. The cliffs are about 700 feet high, and made of sandstone, siltstone, mudstone and shale. The harpist is Tina Mulrooney. She allowed us to take pictures, and her dog seemed so used to the idea that he posed for us.

Blarney Castle - Blarney, County Cork – The castle has accessible rooms and you can ascend the very narrow staircase. At the top you get to kiss the Blarney Stone, if you feel that you need the gift of eloquence. Built before 1200, it is one of the most visited castles in Ireland, but the line moves quickly.

Two Elderly Women - Balbriggan, County Dublin - View from our hotel room. See other entries above.

Cemetery Tower and Cross - Monasterboice Cemetery, County Louth - See above reference about this Irish and Celtic cemetery from 521 AD. This is Muiredach's Cross (18 feet high) which depicts The Last Judgment, The Fall of Man, Moses, David and Goliath and other Biblical scenes.

Man at a Betting Parlour - Balbriggan, County Dublin - View from our hotel room. More description above.

Library at Trinity College II (also see above)– Dublin – Besides housing a copy every book in England and Ireland, one can see on display the Trinity College Harp, known as Brian Boru's Harp. It's an early

Irish wire harp from the 14th or 15th century and was used for the Irish Coat of Arms.

Clock Tower – Belfast, Northern Ireland – Photo taken in Queen's Square, downtown on a walk near our hotel. This tower was built in 1896 and a memorial to Prince Albert. In the tower is a two ton bell, the tower standing 113 feet tall.

Locks on the Lagan Bridge - Belfast, Northern Ireland - These locks are clasped to the safety wall of the bridge, and the keys are thrown into the river. They are commonly known as 'love locks' which sweethearts lock on a bridge or gate to represent their love. The initials or names are often inscribed on the padlock and the key thrown in the water to symbolize unbreakable love.

Hexagonal Basalt Stones - Giant's Causeway, County Antrim – See above entry.

Get your FREE color version of this book in e-reader mobi, epub, or pdf format if you want a color version to read on your computer desktop. Here is the link: *http://www.mikeshawtoday.com/freebook/*

If you have any difficulty downloading from the link, simply send the author an email, and request the version you would like. Send your request to: *freebook@mikeshawtoday.com*

Other Books by Michael Shaw:

The Kids and Teachers Tardigrades Science Project Book
Your Microscope Hobby - How to Make Multi-Colored Filters
Kids & Teachers Tardigrade Quiz and Fact Book
Word Nerd – Things Way Up High Riddle Game Book
Way Up High – Poetry and Photos
Archery Answers – Learn All the Basics Now

8

Screenplay Synopsis

THE ACTUAL SCREENPLAY would take up another 200 pages in the format of this book. Since that would be cost prohibitive for buyers, below you will find a synopsis of the story. You may download the script for free from:

http://www.mikeshawtoday.com/freebook/

```
                    Two Kinds of People

                            by

                     Michael W. Shaw
```

LOGLINE:

After twenty years in prison, an Irishman wrongly convicted of an IRA bombing finds redemption and proves his innocence as he struggles to reconnect with his family.

SYNOPSIS:

Ireland. Country kitchen. McBride Family together. Five year old CELESTE's birthday. MICHAEL, her dad, plans to buy her a puppy. He goes to pick up the puppy and is caught in an IRA bombing. Michael McBride is tried and convicted for the crime.

TWENTY YEARS LATER. Celeste's mom, KATIE, wants Celeste to marry Irish and find the right man. Mom says "Two kinds of people. Those who are Irish, and those who want to be Irish."

Celeste is a nurse. Takes care of a patient named McGILL in the hospital. He's an IRA profiteer. (The bad guy who really committed the bombing.)

Celeste meets KYLE, handsome 20's, at a flea market. She doesn't like him for two reasons: He's from Northern Ireland, and he grew up in America.

Celeste and Kyle meet again on a bus. He is taking his old sick dog to the vet to be put to sleep. Celeste, being a nurse, goes along to be supportive. She starts to like Kyle.

Michael McBride is released from jail early due to the *Good Friday Accord* amnesty release. Kyle goes to Celeste's homecoming party for her dad. Now she really likes Kyle, but afraid to commit because she's afraid of being abandoned again.

Michael struggles to reconnect with his daughter, and make up for lost time with his wife. Since Michael is now an ex-con, he gets the only job available, working for McGill the IRA profiteer. Michael later finds out that it was McGill who put him in jail.

Romance between Celeste and her new flame Kyle. They go with Celeste's parents (Michael & Katie) to a nearby Castle to scatter the ashes of Kyle's dog, over the river. Kyle works in the police station for his dad. Kyle is trying to help Celeste's father, by researching the twenty year old conviction case for clues or errors.

Michael asks Captain FARRELL (the officer who put Michael behind bars) to re-open his case. Farrell is Catholic and is conflicted about going against his police brothers in Northern Ireland. He refuses to re-open the case. Michael says he will prove who really did the bombing by joining the IRA. Farrell threatens to put him in jail again.

We now find out that Capt. Farrell is Kyle's father. Kyle begs his father to help clear Michael's name. Farrell again refuses.

Michael joins McGill's gang and then gets beat up by McGill's thugs. They tell him that Kyle is Farrell's son and disparage Celeste. Michael is furious, and injures McGill, putting him in the hospital.

Celeste has a big fight with Kyle for not telling her that his dad is Captain Farrell who threw her own father in jail. She breaks up with Kyle.

Kyle convinces Celeste that he has a way to prove her father's innocence: Even if she doesn't love him, she should still help her father. Celeste agrees to get blood samples from McGill for DNA while he's in the hospital.

Michael is now arrested once again for his IRA involvement. In the courtroom, Kyle has convinced his dad to testify for Michael (retracting his own former testimony), going against the police force and prosecutor. Testimony reveals that Kyle's dog was the same dog that Michael was supposed to have brought home for Celeste on the day of the bombing. This fact proves Michael's innocence. Michael is exonerated, and McGill is put in cuffs on the spot based on new evidence.

Kyle and Celeste get married, and we close on the reception where they're singing "If You're Irish," all having a great time. Celeste dances with her Dad.

ABOUT THE AUTHOR

Michael Shaw has written several photo-essay books, one winning an award for inspirational poetry. This is his first photo-travelogue book.

His degree in Fine Art from The New York Institute of Technology inspired him to combine art with science in a series of books for teachers and their young scientists to help prepare winning science fair projects.

Mr. Shaw's reproductions of ancient Egyptian Art have been sold at the Metropolitan Museum of Art in New York and at The Field Museum in Chicago. His life-size reproduction of the north wall of King Tutankhamen's tomb was purchased by the Museum at the University of Pennsylvania for permanent display. His commercial art has sold in department stores nationwide, and his art and photography have been featured in books, magazines, and on television.

Printed in Great Britain
by Amazon